T0195787

# You Are Your Best Soul Mate

Learn To Respect Yourself by
The Numbers in Your Life.

NUMEROLOGIST SALLY FAUBION

**BALBOA.**PRESS

A DIVISION OF HAY HOUSE

Balboa Press books may be ordered through booksellers or by contacting:

Balboa Press
A Division of Hay House
1663 Liberty Drive
Bloomington, IN 47403
www.balboapress.com
1 (877) 407-4847

Because of the dynamic nature of the Internet, any web addresses or links contained in this book may have changed since publication and may no longer be valid. The views expressed in this work are solely those of the author and do not necessarily reflect the views of the publisher, and the publisher hereby disclaims any responsibility for them.

The author of this book does not dispense medical advice or prescribe the use of any technique as a form of treatment for physical, emotional, or medical problems without the advice of a physician, either directly or indirectly. The intent of the author is only to offer information of a general nature to help you in your quest for emotional and spiritual well-being. In the event you use any of the information in this book for yourself, which is your constitutional right, the author and the publisher assume no responsibility for your actions.

Any people depicted in stock imagery provided by Getty Images are models, and such images are being used for illustrative purposes only. Certain stock imagery © Getty Images.

Print information available on the last page.

ISBN: 978-1-9822-4062-2 (sc)
ISBN: 978-1-9822-4063-9 (e)

Balboa Press rev. date: 12/30/2019

# Contents

# Acknowledgments

I would like to thank Theresa Matthews, Sue LeSeure, and Sushuma for their help with this book.

# Introduction

The day I purchased my first book on numerology was the day I found my true calling. It would be many years later before I would realize that; but it became my one and only hobby, and for the next many years I was studying and practicing numerology. I purchased every book I could find on the subject and began using what I was learning to help me understand my family members and almost anyone else who happened to cross my path who would give me their birth date. Those who know me well are aware of my obsession with numerology. It is a science, a language, a philosophy, and a tool that I enthusiastically use in my everyday life and for my clients.

While still a numerology hobbyist, I had a legal word processing bureau in downtown San Francisco from 1967 to 1985 and hired all my employees using numerology. Those were the days when you could do that without getting approval for using such means for hiring a potential employee. A few of my employees stayed with me for 5 to 10 years, which was for me a testimonial to the numerological qualities associated with those I chose to hire.

As I continued to study and practice numerology, I began to understand the nuances of numbers that were not written in any books. I could see the high side, the low side, and the in-between characteristics of how the people I analyzed lived their lives. I noticed that the majority of people I researched were inclined to take the in-between path, as it is a path for progress yet without the challenges that come with striving for the heights that they are theoretically capable of accomplishing. I wondered whether they might reach for more if they had an understanding of the highest potential of their numbers.

My purpose for writing this book is to inspire the reader to embrace their in-born highest potential, along with learning to have greater appreciation for themselves from the spiritual tenets I have learned that enhanced my personal life and my business practice.

## EACH CHAPTER HOLDS THE KEYS TO A BETTER YOU

CHAPTER ONE explains why you are your only true soul mate. We are all born with different personalities and potentialities. You will learn in this chapter why there is no one but you who really gives you what you need in your life.

There are also helpful concepts that offer why it is important to learn to love yourself, from a soulful standpoint. I have been associated with a spiritual group called "Oneness Blessing" for the past several years and through its teachings I have learned to overcome the blockages that prevented me from being my best. This chapter will offer specific methods for achieving the ability to let go of the past and learn to love the person you came to be. You are never too old to begin!

CHAPTER TWO offers you the ability to easily determine your primary numbers. Also included in this chapter are the names and numbers of famous individuals who have lived their lives on the "high side" of their numbers, along with one or two who resonated to the "lower side." By observing the numbers of these well-known people who have or had your numbers, you may discover that you have many of their same qualities, talents and accomplishments.

CHAPTER THREE offers a few examples of those who have been revered around the world for their exemplary contributions, like Mother Teresa, Nelson Mandela, and Mohammed Ali, and how their numbers played a role in their lives and accomplishments.

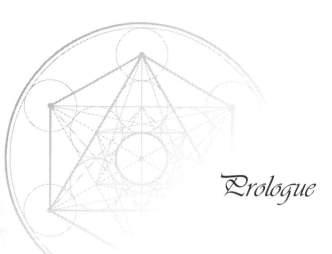

# Prologue

A few years ago, I listened to a DVD titled "The Spirit of Gaia," produced by Mellen-Thomas Benedict. I was inspired by a statement he offered about loving yourself, which became the impetus for this book. In that DVD, Mr. Benedict spoke about aspects of his personal life that were less than inspiring. What turned his life around was an experience he had after being diagnosed with incurable brain cancer at the age of 32. At that time, because he was a struggling artist and had no relations with his family, he checked himself into a hospice to live out what he assumed would be a speedy end to his life. The only request he made of the staff at the hospice was that they would not "pull the plug" on him until they knew for sure he was dead. Honoring his request, they allowed him to lie on the gurney for 6 hours. During this time, he left his body, had an exceptional out-of-body experience, and was able to return from "the other side."

While out of his body for that 6-hour period, Mr. Benedict said he watched as he gave himself brain cancer through his constant negative thinking. He offered that he had been an absolute curmudgeon throughout his young lifetime and had little use for his family and his own life. He learned why that was, along with so many other things, and dedicated himself to sharing these insights to others through CDs, DVDs, and YouTube videos.

There was one outstanding offering that he gave in "The Spirit of Gaia" that inspired me to write the following section of this book. It was that the most important thing you can do to live your best life is to learn to LOVE yourself. By that statement, my hope in writing this book is to influence you to become your BEST SOUL MATE and learn to give yourself greater respect for and acceptance of who you came into this lifetime to be and do.

## Part One

# YOU ARE YOUR BEST SOUL MATE

The following is a compilation of various concepts that have helped me to gain greater understanding of why we, as humans, think the way we think and, more importantly, how we can shift our thought processes to a higher state of consciousness, enabling us to have greater love for ourselves, others, and, indeed, our universe, and in the process, achieve our highest potential.

## POLARITIES

There are multitudes of polarities in life. A few examples are day and night, light and dark, hot and cold, positive and negative, odd and even, love and hate, high and low, and give and take.

Another polarity that exists within every human being is the "Ego-Mind" and the "Soulful-Self." The Ego-Mind is an aspect of our thinking process that dominates all things that gratify the Ego, from winning a board game to owning the Hope diamond. Both examples manifest degrees of drama, and drama is the lifeblood of the Ego-Mind.

The Soulful-Self is the antithesis of the Ego-Mind. It lies within the spirit. When a human being is fully connected to the Soulful-Self, she or he will have much less desire for material things or concern for him/herself. The Soulful-Self emanates and is gratified by compassion and love and helps to move human beings to higher consciousness. The Soulful-Self is notably free of drama.

## HIGHER CONSCIOUSNESS

Higher consciousness is associated with your conscious mind being raised to a higher level or dimension (spiritualists and scientists say we humans can access anywhere from 12 to over 20 dimensions). Many humans are content to stay within the realm of the $3^{rd}$ dimension which is defined as that state of mind where you recognize yourself as an individual human with a past, present, and future and are generally more self-oriented than communally or universally oriented. The $1^{st}$ and $2^{nd}$ dimensions are generally considered those of inanimate objects like crystals ($1^{st}$) and the plant and animal kingdoms ($2^{nd}$). Those who seek higher consciousness are usually involved in mind expanding activities such as meditation, yoga, ecological sustainability, and connecting with groups and programs that offer greater spiritual teachings and knowledge. All contribute to higher consciousness that is characterized by greater awareness of our interconnectedness, the unconscious mind, our spiritual essence, and the profound truths that have existed for thousands of years.

## THE EGO-MIND VS. THE SOULFUL-SELF

### The Ego-Mind

We are all familiar with the Ego-Mind. It is a useful aspect of our personalities when we are challenging ourselves to achieve a goal, whether a career, athletic challenge, monetary goal, or spiritual insight. As an example, most of us have heard of the "One Percent" (the 29,000 individuals who possess over half of all the money on earth at this time). The majority, if not all of those, in that One Percent likely represent the epitome of Ego-Mind. Their unspoken motto might be, "There will never be enough money, possessions, power, and fame," for someone who is wholly connected to the Ego-Mind.

There are many ways to balance the Ego-Mind. The mind can be like a beehive of mental mires with each thought, idea, and emotional state or grievance vying for a prominent position on the mind stage. Daily meditation is one practice that can help to tone down and eventually eliminate the constant brain-chatter and connect you to your "inner self" or "soulful-self." Reading and associating with spiritually-oriented material, practices, and groups is another way to help you gain greater control over your Ego-Mind's manipulative banter.

## The Soulful-Self

Compared to the Ego-Mind, the Soulful-Self can be more difficult to access. We humans, especially in the western world, are constantly inundated with enticements, from magazines, television, and digital advertisements, to bond us to the mindset that having and getting more for ourselves is all that matters.

Nonetheless, we have, at one time or another, all connected with the Soulful-Self, which is referred to by some as the "wee voice within." For example, we occasionally connect with it when experiencing spontaneous selflessness. You might see someone drop something from their purse and run to pick it up and deliver it back to them, or witness someone on the street harming someone or an animal and jump in to stop the offender without a thought to your own safety. Or, consider the first time you held a newborn in your arms and thought about the awesome responsibility of caring for the life of a new human being. Those are all spontaneous selfless experiences. Some are so rare that the people who experience them are labeled heroes. You may have noticed, however, that those involved in selfless acts never consider themselves as heroes but rather, are grateful that they were moved to do what they did.

Another method for connecting with your Soulful-Self is to stay "in the now," a concept promoted by many spiritual icons including Eckhart Tolle and Deepak Chopra. With this practice, which is conceptually simple but surprisingly difficult, the intent is to stay focused on what is happening *right now*, not 5 minutes ago and not what might be planned for later today or next year. This focus can help tame mind chatter and create the quiet needed for the Soulful-Self mind to emerge.

## STAYING IN THE NOW

As expressed before, the Ego-Mind can be The Drama Queen of your life. It can take your mind into exhilarated realms when, for example, you begin reveling in delight with how well things are going. On the other hand, it can take you into greatest depths of depression when facing seemingly overwhelming problems or challenges. The drama is what de-neutralizes life events and produces such highs and lows.

You can better navigate both the ups and downs with a more mellow, comfortable state of mind by embracing spiritual practices such as meditation or prayer. And, "staying in the now" can produce profound life-altering results.

As an example, think of a time when you were a child lying in the tall grass, gazing up at the clouds as they passed by. In those times, you relaxed into the moment, into the now, losing yourself in the beauty of the clouds and letting your imagination float into the sky and play with the animal shapes you were seeing. You may recall rising after a while, happy and ready to return home to enjoy the rest of your day. Children have an easier time connecting with that state because they usually have fewer cares and concerns than their parents or other adults.

Another good example of staying in the now is achieved by liking what you are doing. When you are enjoying yourself, whether that involves your job, writing a book or poem, gardening, or working a crossword puzzle, you can move into a trance-like mode of engagement when you are fully into the circumstances at hand. You may even experience the bodily reaction of a startle or flinch when someone interrupts you when so absorbed. That is another good example of what being in the now can be like.

Staying in the now doesn't mean that you wander about with no thoughts or cares or concerns. It means being interested enough in what you are doing that thoughts of the past and future are not relevant. A Peruvian shaman recently put it this way:

*"The past is what has already happened. Thus, you can see it and it is, if anything, in front of you...not behind you if you choose to focus on it. The future has not yet happened. One cannot 'see' it and so it is figuratively 'behind' you. Only the present is real and actionable. And the present is this very moment."*

The feeling of being at One with everything occurs when you have gained control over the Ego-Mind and are living mostly in the now. We humans experience many *in the now* periods throughout our day. As expressed above, this state can occur when you are focusing exclusively on one thing, such as reading this paragraph right now. It may also emerge as an epiphany or awareness that leaves you feeling inexplicably joyful. These are times when you are connecting with your inner self – your soul, the part of your "self" where selfless love resides.

## ENERGY

We are often creating, whether it is a work product, an ambiance for the party we are giving, or simply the thoughts we have about who we are or the quality of life we are having. When you are in the now and free of drama, the energy you bring to what you are creating can be much more balanced and positive than when the Ego-Mind is operating with its attendant dramatic energy.

While not an authority on quantum physics, I have read that quantum physicists have come to understand that energy exists in multiple states at one time (both wave and particle) and at different frequencies. Observe it with a certain instrument, and it is a particle. Observe it in another way, and it is a wave. The take home message is that **what you observe becomes real**. This is the fundamental hypothesis of quantum physics that explains the law of attraction. Expressed more simply, what you perceive is what you receive.

Athletes are familiar with manifesting a particular outcome when running a race, challenging an opponent, or climbing a mountain. A champion athlete is always visualizing her/his performance at an optimal level. The athlete must of course be "in the now" so that his or her mind is focused on the present moment, but they are also observing, feeling, and practicing the energy of the outcome they want, such as summiting a mountain or winning a race.

## CAUSE AND EFFECT

You may already be familiar with the law of Cause and Effect. It is another universal scientific principle that can help you to understand why your thoughts, actions, and words matter on a day-to-day basis.

**Cause** is the producer of an **effect**,
while an **effect** is produced by a **cause**.

Every thought, action, and word, we speak can have an effect on our lives. Many have heard about, read, and perhaps followed the philosophy behind *The Secret* which was a book introduced with great success in 2006 by author Rhonda Byrne. The emphasis in that book focused on positive thinking. We now know that there is a great difference between the positive thinking done by the Ego-Mind versus that of the Soulful-Self. The truth behind positive thinking can lead to achieving much greater abundance in life by learning to focus on positive thinking that emanates from your Soulful-Self.

Regardless of whether you are working with the tenets of *The Secret* or *Think and Grow Rich* by Napoleon Hill, the main theme is to focus on a goal in order to manifest a personal desire and to do it from a deeper connection (Soulful-Self) through prayer or sincere conviction. Just wanting it or feeling you deserve it without intention and conviction would likely not deliver the desired results.

## SELF LOVE

Learning to love "YOU" is the first and foremost requirement for achieving the highest potential of your numbers and attracting to you everything you came into being to receive. When you are able to appreciate your personal existence from a Self Love posture, intentionally and purposefully, you will experience the essence of the Soulful-Self and open the floodgates to all your hopes and desires.

There are those on this earth who have already risen to the highest levels of consciousness through great discipline and application of certain tenets. The Buddha and the Dalai Lama are two spiritual icons who are known to have achieved exalted levels of awareness, selflessness and compassion. Today, ordinary people are acquiring a state close to that even without studying spiritual tenets or practicing esoteric and metaphysical disciplines through spontaneous epiphanies and out-of-body experiences, along with other spiritually-oriented practices. We are being given the opportunity to rise to higher levels of consciousness simply by becoming aware of the triggers that provoke a less than charitable nature in ourselves and others. This "rising up of consciousness" is a natural consequence of delving into one's unconscious and conscious minds to uncover and heal judgments, unproductive beliefs, hatred, and prejudices that do not serve our highest potentials. Learning your personal numerological composition can also inspire you to aspire toward your in-born highest potential.

# FORGIVENESS

Over my many years of having researched and analyzed thousands of numerological charts of my clients and public figures, I have found that everyone, including me, has what I call "pockets of challenge" in their charts. Through my spiritual studies I learned that everything happens for a reason, so I therefore began to analyze my own chart during past challenging periods to determine if I gained anything positive from them. Inevitably, I found that every difficult challenging "pocket" I had enabled me to rise to a new level of understanding, compassion, and empathy for myself and others. I also strongly suspect that I might not have developed these insights as quickly, if ever, without those experiences.

Typically, people think of rendering forgiveness in relation to an offense perpetrated upon them or of the offender, or for doing something shameful themselves. Forgiveness is essentially the pathway to loving all that is. When you can love all that IS, you are in a much better position to reach their highest potential. Unless you have risen to the heights of the Dalai Lama and those comparable, this is a most difficult requisite for attaining and maintaining "higher consciousness."

As an example, something as forgivable as being snubbed by someone you care for can cause some to become virtually neurotic over such an oversight. Or perhaps you didn't get the raise in salary you expected for your efforts, and become despondent because of that. If you can spontaneously decide to forgive those involved in whatever is causing you untoward feelings and see the plausible "rightness" of what occurred, you will instantly be taken to a higher consciousness level. Or, by allowing yourself to accept what has occurred without resentment indicates that you have already arrived at that higher level.

Forgiveness is a gift not only for the one carrying the grievance, but also for the offender. Everything is energy. Grievances lower your energy level and must be released to achieve your highest potential. Being in the now, self-love and forgiveness, along with gaining an understanding of your highest potential through numerology, offer a direct route to that destination.

## WHO IS YOUR SOUL MATE?

While most of you know or at least have a good idea what a "soul mate" is, Dictionary.com defines it as: A person with whom you have a strong affinity, shared values and tastes, and often a romantic bond.

I suggest, however, that **YOU** are your best soul mate and in keeping with that premise, the above definition should change as follows: YOU, as your BEST Soul Mate, have a natural affinity with your values and tastes, along with an innate Supreme LOVE that enables you to bond with your soul and thereby attract to you all the best experiences, people, and things for you in this lifetime.

Love must start in our homes, and I suggest our true "home" is love of SELF. That person with whom you have the strongest affinity, shared values and tastes, and often a "loving" bond is YOU.

Here are a few questions to ask yourself that might help you understand why YOU are your BEST Soul Mate:

1.  Whose breath sustains your life?
2.  Whose heart do you feel beating?
3.  Who takes your actions?

4. Who makes your decisions? [You may confront the fact that you have given decision-making to another].
5. Whose hopes and dreams can you best manifest?
6. Whose childhood most affects your life?
7. Whose feelings affect you more than anyone else's?
8. Whose thoughts do you conjure up on a constant basis?

You, and only you, have the ultimate power to change your life for the better, to make decisions fully aligned with your values and dreams, AND to take the actions required to follow through with those decisions.

At different times in your life, you may have sought counseling to help overcome certain challenges, but that may have been money wasted if you were not ready to hear the advice being given. Even when it's very apparent to you that certain advice would be good to follow, until you are ready to truly love and believe in your higher potential, it may be difficult to follow through.

You, and only you, can love as you love, and you are IT when it comes to loving yourself. Loving oneself doesn't mean ego love but "soulful love." Ego love is usually based on extraneous elements of your life, such as your physical appearance, educational achievements, job status, and material possessions. Soulful love is inside yourself, always present, always offering guidance. When one allows soulful love to captain their life and keep ego love firmly in the co-pilot's seat, one can achieve their highest potential. Ego is not bad, it just should not be in charge. It gets one to the gym, making sales calls, writing books, etc., and when it is used to give you fortitude and perseverance, it is a major plus.

## WHAT IS SOULFUL LOVE?

Soulful love is love that starts at home. What does it look and feel like when YOU are your BEST Soul Mate? When you TRULY love yourself, you love the complete package. You love that you are perfectly imperfect and imperfectly perfect. You love that you are fearless climbing a cliff yet uncomfortable driving in traffic or dynamic in one-on-one conversations, but unsure in a party environment. And the natural, unavoidable consequence of this kind of love is that it spills over into your life as you begin to see, appreciate, embrace, and love the similar imperfect perfection of your friends, communities, and life in general.

You do not have to have full command of Soulful Love to glean value from your numbers. My many, many readings suggest, however, that for many, seeking insight through numerology readings goes hand in hand with an unconscious, innate desire to deepen their love of themselves.

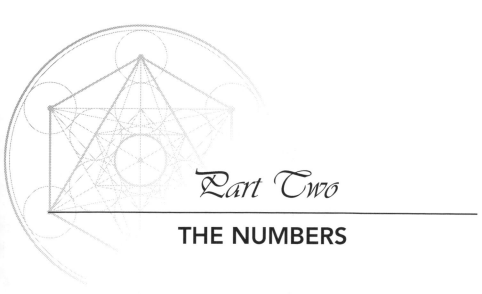

# *Part Two*

## THE NUMBERS

**Numbers based on their numerological meaning can help you gain greater respect and appreciation for the grand person you came to this earth plane to be.**

When I became a professional numerologist, numbers soon began to jump out at me from everywhere. I began to understand what Stephen Hawking and others have stated—that this is a universe based upon mathematics. Every atom has its own rate of vibration and path of oscillation, and when these combine in due proportion to each other, they create sacred geometry, which in turn becomes the structure of all matter. Thus, the instinct to associate numbers with humans is supported by the physics and mathematics of the universe.

The history of numerology predates Pythagoras, the renowned Greek mathematician and philosopher who lived circa 500 BC. It is recorded that Pythagoras presented the concept that "all things in the universe can be reduced to numbers" and that "all numbers resonate the profound forces of the universe," namely, energy forces.

Pythagoras spent thirty years traveling throughout eastern cultures studying ancient occult traditions. In Greece, he studied the Oracle of Delphi, and the mysteries of Isis in Egypt. He also received special tutelage in Persia by the Zoroastrians about the doctrines of the Magi. In Babylonia, he learned about the "Science of Numbers" from the Chaldeans, and he also journeyed to India where he gathered knowledge from Brahman priests about the sacred tenets of the Hindu Vedas. On yet another leg of his travels, he explored the secret traditions of the Kabbalah from ancient Hebrew rabbis.

Pythagoras, considered the Father of Numerology in the western world, used various aspects of each of those ancient doctrines to render "western" numerology. Some of those ancient sciences are still in use today, like the Science of Numbers by the Chaldeans and the Jewish Kabbalah. The Pythagorean method is, however, the most accepted process used by modern-day numerologists and it is used in this book to bring to light the personal qualities and traits of individuals as revealed by each reader's specific numbers.

There are various theories as to how each person comes to possess certain numbers. One is that the numbers (destiny, life path, etc.) are a function of the energetic vibrations emblazoned on one's etheric body at birth. The etheric body is the first layer in the human energy field, more commonly referred to as the "aura." It is in immediate contact with the physical body and interfaces between the body and "higher" bodies, like spirit guides and guardian angels. Every human has numeric vibrations that reflect the positive and negative charges associated with the different facets of individualized consciousness and these are deeply correlated with a person's birth date and name.

When you think about it, numbers are ubiquitous in our lives. Society has inundated us with numbers, not only during our school years and in business, but also in our daily lives. Think about all the numbers in your life: your Social Security number, driver's license, credit cards, bank accounts, computer and ATM pins, passwords, addresses and phone numbers, to say nothing of constantly consulting your watches, clocks, calendars and calculators.

Those in science express that "numbers are the language of the universe" and on the earth, numbers are also the language of computers in zeros and ones! This book offers your "numbers" for personal identification purposes and also can help you to learn to appreciate and respect who you are and have come into being on this planet.

## THE THREE PRIMARY NUMBER VIBRATIONS

After more than 40 years of learning, researching, analyzing, and creating apps and other products associated with numerology, I came to the conclusion that, regardless of what anyone says about the metaphysical sciences, I know first-hand that numerology is an absolute science, albeit mystical, that offers information and insight into our lives, personalities and desires. The numbers are imprinted energetically in the individuals auras of each human being on this earth.

I am often told that my readings are "spot on" despite doing almost all reading by phone. I read strictly from the numbers and letters on numerological charts, and the software, which compiles each numerological chart, is my own composition.

Over the years, I have expanded my repertoire to include knowledge and understanding of the numbers that aren't in any book on the market today. I developed this information by analyzing and researching the 99 primary numbers incessantly, and from sources, I believe, beyond this realm of existence.

I offer the above because I want to stress that what I have learned is that there is wisdom in all aspects of your life that it suggests YOU are the one who has chosen your parents, your name, and your birthdate, and YOU are the one who has given yourself everything from blessings to challenges in your numerological chart to enable you to connect with your soul. As expressed earlier, our greatest growth occurs when we go through the challenges we face, and the tougher the challenge, the greater the opportunity to achieve understanding, compassion, and empathy for others. In other words, the challenges you face in this life are really the greatest gifts you gave yourself for your own spiritual evolution.

I offer the following definitions of the three primary numerological vibrations in everyone's life with the most positive definitions and refrain from offering the negative qualities that may show up when one is not practicing soulful love. I believe it is important that YOU, being your best soul mate, learn who you came onto this earth to be from the most positive aspects of the numbers you assigned to yourself.

Once you have calculated your own numbers, and read the definitions, I suggest that you use your findings as goals for your future, if you haven't already mastered the qualities offered.

## CHARACTER, PERSONALITY AND DESTINY

The **CHARACTER** number is derived from the full name you were given at birth, specifically, the name on your birth certificate. This number offers **WHAT YOU BROUGHT WITH YOU INTO THIS LIFETIME TO HELP YOU FROM A CHARACTER STANDPOINT**. It plays its most significant role in your work or profession and in your social life.

The **PERSONALITY** number is derived from of the day of the month you were born, e.g., the 2nd, the 13th, the 24th, the 30th. This number vibration is representative of your "inside" personality. It is the personality you exhibit to those who are closest to you – your family members and intimate friends and associates. It is **WHO YOU ARE WHEN BEING THE MOST AUTHENTIC YOU.**

The **DESTINY** number is determined by adding together all the numbers in your birth date and reducing the compound number derived therefrom to a single digit.

As the word "Destiny" implies, it represents **WHAT YOU CAME INTO THIS LIFE TO ACCOMPLISH; WHAT CAREERS ARE BEST SUITED TO YOU; WHO YOU GRAVITATE TOWARD AND RETAIN AS FRIENDS AND MATES; WHAT ACTIVITIES OR SOCIAL ATMOSPHERE YOU MOST DESIRE; AND THE WHO, WHAT, AND WHERE ARE YOUR PREFERENCES IN YOUR SURROUNDINGS.**

## CALCULATING YOUR CHARACTER NUMBER

<u>Note</u>: **You can learn how to calculate your own three primary numbers, or you can use an easier method by downloading my App titled "Cosmic Mates," which is available for iOs and Android devices. The app will do all the calculations for you and offer even more qualities associated with your numerological profile.**

The numbers 1 through 9 are the primary numbers used in numerology to explain qualities, traits, characteristics, and the destiny of a person by numerology. The formula for finding the character number is simple. One simply adds together the numbers associated with the letters of the name from birth and reduces that total to a single digit.

*IMPORTANT:* The "name from birth" must be the FULL name from birth – first, middle (if any) and last or surname. If one or more of the name numbers reduces to the number 11 or 22, then those numbers should not be reduced to the lower denomination. These double-digit numbers are classified as Master Numbers. The 11 is the higher vibration of the number 2, and 22 is the higher vibration of the number 4. Master Numbers are found in the charts of those who are here to express a higher consciousness approach and to give more to their fellow humans than what is expected from someone with a 2 or 4 "destiny number. "

The following grid shows which number correlates which each letter of the alphabet:

| 1 | 2 | 3 | 4 | 5 | 6 | 7 | 8 | 9 |
|---|---|---|---|---|---|---|---|---|
| a | b | c | d | e | f | g | h | i |
| j | k | l | m | n | o | p | q | r |
| s | t | u | v | w | x | y | z |   |

The Character Number designates the qualities you brought with you into this life that expresses your mental and moral qualities especially in your work and social life. You will use this number vibration in your home life, too, but usually only in an officiating capacity.

The following example of Nelson Mandela is used for the purpose of illustrating someone who led an exemplary life exhibiting the highest qualities of his numbers.

## NELSON ROLIHLAHLA MANDELA

**NELSON =** 5+5+3+1+6+5 = 25, 2+5 = 7

**ROLIHLAHLA =** 9+6+3+9+8+3+1+8+3+1 = 51 and 5+1 = 6

**MANDELA =** 4+1+5+4+5+3+1 = 23, 2+3 = 5

7 + 6 + 5 = 18 AND 1+8 = <u>9</u>

The number 9 is Mr. Mandela's "Character" number. This is the number that expresses what Mr. Mandela brought from past incarnations into this life to help him in this one. The 9 is the number of a very old soul. It indicates someone who can draw from his past life knowledge more readily than others. The 9 is the "Universal Humanitarian" and Mr. Mandela certainly lived up to that number by setting an example for the world with his stalwart stand for equality, justice, compassion, and forgiveness for the people of South Africa.

# CHARACTER NUMBER VIBRATION DEFINITIONS
### (Who You Could Be In Business and Socially)

No. 1: An ambitious, original, innovative, achievement-oriented, courageous, individualistic, trail-blazing leader.

No. 2: Agreeable, adaptable, diplomatic, modest, conciliatory, peacemaking, supportive, ambassador of and for the people.

No. 3: An optimistic, imaginative, original, inspirational, literate, creative, artistic, tasteful communicator.

No. 4: A candid, conscientious, reliable, hard-working, forthright, practical, honest, pragmatic, systematic orchestrator.

No. 5: A socially charming, enthusiastic, energized, versatile, progressive, persuasive, independent promoter and trendsetter.

No. 6: An altruistic, responsible, principled seeker of fairness and justice, managerial, go-the-extra-mile humanitarian.

No. 7: A reserved, wise, analytical, patient, dignified, truth-seeking, broad-minded erudite, unique visionary.

No. 8: An exemplary, principled, refined, diplomatic, enterprising, far-sighted, quality operator, teacher-of-teachers and class act.

No. 9: An astute, modest, aristocratic, socially adept, hospitable, enlightened, impassioned "universal" humanitarian.

No. 11: A clairvoyant, empathetic, intuitive, inspiring, progressive, inventive, ministerial counselor or leader.

No. 22: A high-minded, constructive, organized, humane, ingenious, spiritually oriented, masterful visionary

## CALCULATING YOUR PERSONALITY NUMBER

The Personality Number beats the drum of your real, "behind-the-scenes" personality. It defines your *inside* world – who you are at home and with intimate friends and family members.

Figuring out your personality number is very simple. It is simply the day of the month on which you were born, meaning the 1st, the 13th, the 23rd, etc.

You are not required to reduce your birthday number to a single digit. The following definitions include the compound dates.

## PERSONALITY NUMBER VIBRATION DEFINITIONS

1: You are creative, innovative, and blessed with exceptional organizational skills. Your fashion sense and style showcase your originality. Once you are committed to a goal, your single-minded focus and determination carry you into the winner's circle. Self-reliant and confident, you may find it difficult to take orders from others. Your highly independent, take-charge nature is tempered by a delightful sense of humor. Your ethics tend to be practical and your values are traditional.

2: Your helpful, conscientious, and capable nature renders you an indispensable "right hand" to anyone with whom you work or live. Your intrinsic desire for harmony and your ability to comprehend both sides of any issue make you an exceptional arbitrator/

peacemaker. Quick-witted and socially adept, you are a born crowd-pleaser. Naturally nurturing, you derive great joy from hosting get-togethers for friends and family. You are a kind parent, a considerate mate, and a great friend.

3: Your eloquent, silver-tongued wit, and inimitable charm give you a definite social advantage. A vivid imagination and captivating storytelling abilities make you a natural-born entertainer. You like using your brain rather than your brawn in a career endeavor and, if inspired by a project or idea, your enthusiasm is boundless. An optimist by nature, you retain your youthful demeanor throughout your lifetime. You were born to be a star among your peers!

4: You are a "Rock of Gibraltar" whose word is as good as gold. Always a tireless and conscientious worker, you are detail-oriented and organized. Strong principles and common sense contribute to your stable character. Confidence in your own point of view and a love of debate are empowered by your excellent memory and penchant for collecting facts. You like research and analysis. You have difficulty releasing anything that is bothersome to you until you have solved whatever is causing your angst. An exceptionally good and giving friend, you are also a gift to anyone who is lucky enough to employ you.

5: Your intelligent, enthusiastic, and friendly personality makes it easy for you to inspire and motivate others, and you have a natural gift of persuasion. Progressive and curious, you are always tuned in to the latest news, fashions, and social trends. Freedom of action, speech, and thought are essential to your wellbeing. Brimming with energy and adept at multitasking, you accomplish everything you set out to do with unparalleled speed and agility. Your charismatic savoir-faire gives you a star-like appeal and you collect many and different friends and fans as you are constantly expanding your horizons.

6: You are a lover of nature and the home, and you have a knack for making almost any environment more appealing and livable. A superb host/hostess, you take pleasure in delivering contentment and comfort to your guests. Your strong values and principles are solidly cast at an early age. Idealistic and caring, you are a champion of fairness and justice. You have a strong humanitarian calling, especially for helping those who are least capable of helping themselves. You are one of the best friends anyone can have, and you are a good and loyal companion.

7: You are individualistic, independent, and wise, and you have an unquenchable thirst for knowledge. Your views of life are conservative in some ways and liberal in others. A dedicated perfectionist, you can master anything that holds your interest. You tend to be reserved and private and require a place of solitude to reflect and recharge your energy. Your enigmatic character makes it easy for you to be outstanding among your peers. You are the perfect confidant because you listen well and never tell. Your friends and companions tend to be unique and unusual.

8: You are a born executive. Like a military general or a stage director, you can orchestrate, organize, and delegate with aplomb. You are the class act that sets the example for others to emulate. Quality is your benchmark, and you have the "buyer's eye." Many born on the 8th are connoisseurs of the arts. You know the value of money, and your talent for getting the best deal is aided by your calculating mind and a desire for quality over quantity. Although you are somewhat hard-nosed in your political and philosophical views, you can be a champion for the underdog. Your favorite friends tend to be like you and usually share your same values.

9: You are multi-talented, creative, competent, and your best qualities shine when you are in a position of leadership. Eloquence is one of your greatest assets, and you can be very persuasive when the spirit moves you. You have a taste for the best, from apparel and accessories to food and travel venues. Your desire for independence shares equal billing with your need for a stable home life. You also possess a heightened awareness and you are in your true element when being of service to others. You are also a quality friend and committed mate.

10: You are sensitive, considerate, and kind. Self-sufficient and responsible, with a strong take-charge nature, you usually find yourself in positions of authority and leadership. A natural optimist, you tend to see the positive in most situations. Your political and philosophical views are generally broad and open-minded. Always desiring to learn new things, you especially enjoy associating with people whose backgrounds and interests differ from your own. You are a gentle leader, loyal friend, and conscientious, considerate mate and parent.

11: You are gifted with extraordinary intelligence, originality, and an abundance of creativity. Being a good listener, you tend to attract people with problems. You naturally assume the 'big shoulders" role because you enjoy helping others and sharing the pearls of your innate wisdom. Whether conservative or liberal, you will take an unyielding stand for causes in which you believe. You are born to be a light of inspiration and enlightenment for many. Your friendships are enduring, and you are an interesting and inspiring companion.

12: You have a charming, clever, good-natured personality and a great sense of humor. Self-expression is a must for you, and your gifted imagination and creativity give you a natural artistic bent. You tend to attract strong, individualistic friends who enjoy your easy-going, independent nature. Travel and meeting new and different people are essential to your happiness. You will likely retain your youthful appearance and attitude forever! You are a good and loyal friend and a fascinating companion.

13: You are independent, creative, and down-to-earth. A loyal and devoted friend, your word is as good as gold. When pursuing a goal, your tenacity, fortitude, and organizational skills are extraordinary. Collecting facts and debating absolutely everything comes naturally to you. Your security-oriented nature thrives on a happy home life, and you are most content when engaged in a hobby or personal project. Your resolve, dedication, and determination are the qualities that ensure your life's dreams will come true!

14: You have an abundance of energy and a computer-like mind. A powerful, charismatic communicator, you speak your mind in a forthright, honest fashion. Your freedom-oriented character adapts easily to all types of people, places, and things. Your talents are many and you have an exceptionally creative imagination. You are a good organizer and tend to prosper most when managing your own affairs. You collect all manner of friends and can be an appealing and captivating companion.

15: You are independent and freedom-oriented but also a lover of the home. You are at your best and most fulfilled when helping people and/or animals and working in nature. Highly principled, you have a profound sense of fairness and, if politically or emotionally moved, you can be a dedicated champion of humanitarian causes. You have a conscientious, responsible attitude toward your home, family and community, and you are willing to sacrifice for those you love. You are a dedicated and loyal friend.

16: You are curious and contemplative, and you require time alone to sort through and analyze your mind's constant flow of inspiration. The mysterious and clandestine attract you, partly due to your unquenchable thirst for knowledge. A penchant for privacy gives you an alluring mystique. Your innate genius and mental prowess help to ensure success wherever you seek it. You are a perfectionist in your work endeavors, and a supreme confidant and friend.

17: You are intelligent, ambitious, and possess enough energy and vitality to run a country! Quality is your maxim, and you have a natural eye for excellence and beauty. Your common sense, efficiency, and organizational abilities help you to rise to positions of authority and respect. Your values are traditional, and you nurture close family ties and loyal friendships. You were born under a star of good fortune that delivers its rewards in direct proportion to your industry and integrity.

18: You are multi-talented and possess uncommon wisdom, strength, and courage. Your astute use of words, inimitable charm, and willingness to take risks are assets that make you stand out among your peers. You are capable of far-reaching compassion and understanding of your fellow humans, especially the helpless and suffering. Once you catch the "travel bug," it is essential to your happiness that you incorporate a consistent amount of travel and change into your lifestyle. You possess qualities that enable you to achieve great things in your lifetime!

19: Your adventuresome spirit and individualism make you yearn for variety and change. Your passion, tenacity, and incredible resilience enable you to meet any challenge and prevail. Verbally persuasive, you easily sway others to your way of thinking. Your intelligent, witty nature makes you an interesting and entertaining companion, and you attract strong and abiding friendships throughout your lifetime. Your leadership qualities accord you a sure-fire road to success!

20: Your warm, congenial nature makes it easy for you to collect and retain many friends. You can be like a human barometer, easily sensing the moods and attitudes of everyone in your environment. A promoter of harmony and camaraderie, you are a natural peacemaker. Your gentle, sensitive spirit requires retreats to quiet places to revitalize and maintain your sense of balance. Thoughtful, diplomatic, and astute, you are endowed with the attributes of a benevolent ambassador and a great friend!

21: You are good natured, generous, and charming. You are also an exceptional host/hostess, and you thoroughly enjoy entertaining and being entertained. Your delightful, sometimes dramatic, repartee makes it easy for you to steal the spotlight wherever you go. Optimistic and a bit of an idealist, you are attracted to concepts and schemes that are exciting, challenging, and sometimes risky. Your strong artistic and musical inclinations attract you to beauty, quality, and the performing arts. You are a fun and easy-going companion.

22: You are sensitive, energetic, strong-willed, and logical. You enjoy lively debates on virtually any topic. Your clever intellect, wry wit, and ability to make others laugh give you great social appeal. You are routine-oriented and desire orderly, functional surroundings. Although you tend to be conservative and conventional, you can also be idealistic and occasionally get carried away by your dreams. However, you usually accomplish what you set out to do because of your willingness to work hard. Good home and family relations give you a sense of worthiness and security.

23: You possess a fun-loving, freedom-oriented spirit. A turbo-charged force within you keeps you in the know and on the go! Your quick intelligence delivers original ideas and views, and you are an excellent problem-solver. You are open-minded and enjoy learning about life from different perspectives. You are not bound by convention or tradition and, because of your good-natured and upbeat demeanor, you gain respect from your peers. Your congenial personality makes it easy for you to gather and keep friends.

24: You are intelligent, charming and witty, and your sensual nature draws you to anything that appeals to the senses. Sound principles and ethical standards support your orderly, honest, and committed nature, and you have a strong sense of fairness and justice. Upholding family and social traditions is important to you and spending time in your home gives you great personal satisfaction. You were born to champion causes that help to make the world a better place. You are a good and loyal friend and companion.

25: You are charming and intelligent, and your desire for knowledge is equal only to your reservoir of innate wisdom. You are also trustworthy, loyal, honest, and prone to perfectionism. You possess uncanny intuitive powers and can readily perceive the moods and motives of others. You also have a quiet side that requires time alone to recharge, and art endeavors or sports can serve as relaxing and enjoyable outlets. Your easy-going nature makes you a favorite with family and friends.

26: You are a master of organization and are fully capable of carrying out the grand plans and ideas your fertile mind devises. Your steadfast, resolute personality is in command of every mission you assume. Highly intelligent, with strong leadership abilities, you are never content in a subordinate position and usually find a way to have your own business. Your insistence on quality is complemented by your natural "buyer's eye." Your strong humanitarian leanings make you ever ready to lend a helping hand.

27: You are naturally compassionate and empathetic, and you possess a depth of understanding and perceptivity. Your capabilities and interests are vast and varied, and you can accomplish anything you set your mind to. The biggest challenge you face is deciding which of your many talents to emphasize. Your genteel charm and eloquence enable you to impress others and mix easily with everyone. You were born to be a humanitarian and a terrific friend.

28: You are charming, diplomatic, an achiever, and a leader. You attract friends from all walks of life. Courageous and bold, self-possessed yet reserved, you are an independent risk taker who desires personal recognition and a high degree of autonomy. You possess sound principles and a strong-willed, freedom-oriented nature that helps you to accomplish your many and varied goals. Your compassionate and affectionate nature makes you an easy touch for anyone who needs your aid.

29: You are nurturing, gentle, and sensitive. You enjoy learning and can inspire others with your abundance of knowledge and insight. Your unbridled enthusiasm and leadership abilities inspire others to join your cause. You frequently become the 'big shoulders" to others, listening to their problems and helping them with your caring and astute advice. You are a natural punster and enjoy entertaining your friends and family. Your generous, peacemaking nature readily gains you the respect and appreciation of many.

30: You are intelligent, creative, fun-loving, and blessed with a wonderful sense of humor. Expressing yourself is essential to your happiness. Manual labor is definitely not your calling, but when you are involved in something you enjoy, you can exercise great effort and discipline. Highly companionable, your natural charm and charisma draw a multitude of admirers to you. You are an endless source of fun, pleasure, and inspiration to everyone you know!

31: You are creative, innovative, hard-working, and responsible. Even though you are a creature of habit, orderliness, and routine, you also have a highly independent, nonconformist streak. You enjoy traveling and learning about different cultures, but you also delight in the quiet comforts of your home. A loyal, dependable friend and mate, you are always ready with a helping hand and an understanding heart.

## CALCULATING YOUR DESTINY NUMBER

The following is the addition process to follow with your own birth date. We'll use Nelson Mandela's birthdate, July 18, 1918, as an example:

7 (July) + 1+8 (18th) + 1+9+1+8 = 35 and 3+5 = 8

Mr. Mandela's Destiny number was an 8. The Number 8 as a Destiny number implies that Mr. Mandela came onto this earth plane to be an exemplar, a patriarch, a producer/ director, a general, a leader of leaders, a teacher of teachers, and a class act. His history has defined him in those triumphant terms.

## DESTINY NUMBER VIBRATION DEFINITIONS

**Destiny Number 1:** This is the path of the risk-taker, the entrepreneur, and the wholly independent trailblazer. Having a One Destiny, you came into this life to be as autonomous as possible and this Destiny number ensures that you have what it takes to call your own shots and run your own show.

One-Destiny people are powerful, independent, charming, and loaded with innate talent. You are the most original, pioneering, and innovative of all the destiny numbers. You also have minds like steel traps regarding subject matter that interests you. You can be formidable debaters should the opportunity arise. It is well known by your friends and followers that you are also the most competitive people on the planet because of your winner-takes-all attitude. It is an understatement to say that you do not like to lose at anything. In fact, most of you won't even participant in a game – be it a board game or something more competitive like a team sport, tennis, or golf – unless you think you can outmaneuver or outplay the other players. It's reasonable to say that when you are personally motivated to win, you can virtually flatten anything or anyone who might try to impede your ultimate goal. You can be an indomitable force when you WANT to be.

You also tend to collect friends from your past such as grade-school and high-school chums and are loyal to those friendships for a lifetime. You are also collectors of gadgets. Most of you have a strong linear leaning and enjoy taking things apart and putting them back together again or starting from scratch, figuring out how to operate even the most difficult concepts and gadgets.

**Some famous people who have exhibited superlative abilties with the Destiny Number ONE:**

**SCIENTISTS**: Isaac Newton, Nikola Tesla, Carl Sagan, Michio Kaku, Alfred Nobel, René Descartes, Ernest Rutherford, Blaise Pascal, Maria Montessori

**FINE ARTISTS:** Max Ernst, Amedeo Modigliani, Jean Millet, Georges Seurat, Emil Nolde, Eugene Delacroix, Camille Corot

**WRITERS:** William Shakespeare, Herman Melville, Walt Whitman, Leo Tolstoy, Anton Chekhov, Miguel Cervantes, Somerset Maugham, Aldous Huxley, e. e. Cummings, Dr. Seuss, Truman Capote, Maya Angelou, Tom Wolfe, Ernest Hemingway, Salman Rushdie

**ATHLETES:** Frank Gifford, Johnny Unitas, Jim Brown, Jimmy Connors, Shaq O'Neal, Magic Johnson, LeBron James, Tiger Woods, Sheryl Swoopes, Liz Cambage, Jewell Loyd, Courtney Vandersloot, Kevin Durant

**MUSICIANS/SINGERS:** Noel Coward, Placido Domingo, Sarah Vaughn, Chuck Berry, Bruce Springsteen, Yo Yo Ma, Judy Collins, Marvin Gaye, Al Jarreau, Ringo Starr, David Cosby, Janis Joplin, Alice Cooper, James Taylor, Ozzy Osbourne, Billy Joel, Sting, Lady Gaga, Shakira, Marvin Gaye, Eminem, Sting, James Taylor, Al Green, Lady Gaga, Cyndi Lauper, Janis Joplin

**COMEDIANS:** Milton Berle, Rodney Dangerfield, Carl Reiner, Jerry Lewis, Carol Burnett, George Carlin, David Letterman, Ray Romano, Chris Farley, Aziz Ansari, Tim Allen, Bernie Mac

**FASHION DESIGNERS:** Christian Dior, Edith Head, Yves St. Laurent, Ralph Lauren, Calvin Klein, John Galliano, Christian

Lacroix, Salvatore Ferragamo, Emilio Pucci, Elsa Schiaparelli, Thierry Mugler

**FAMOUS CHEFS:** Charlie Chaplin, Ferran Adria, Marc Veyrat, Madhur Jaffrey, Curtis Stone, Pierre Gagnaire

**ACTORS:** Sophia Loren, Sally Field, Holly Hunter, Raquel Welch, Gwyneth Paltrow, Charlize Theron, Kate Winslet, Scarlett Johansson, Daniel Day Lewis, Tom Hanks, Samuel L. Jackson, Jack Nicholson, George Clooney, Tom Cruise, Bradley Cooper, Spencer Tracy, Christopher Plummer, Sean Connery, Hugh Jackman, Charlie Chaplin, Ingrid Bergman, Lynn Redgrave, Michelle Pfeiffer, Holly Hunter, Halle Berry, Angie Harmon, Kate Winslet

**DESTINY NUMBER 2:** This is the path of the homemaker, the team player, the caretaker and the collector. If you have a Two Destiny, you are warm, affectionate, compassionate, and exhibit a depth of understanding when someone comes to you for consolation or counseling. You will easily set aside your own desires or needs for someone else's and you enjoy giving more than receiving. This is the most nurturing of all the numbers, and its vibration summons forth the impulses of a doting mother or protective father. Most everyone with a Two Destiny is gentle, considerate, diplomatic, sympathetic, and a natural caretaker. As a consequence, your life is filled with many friends and social engagements. Those who are fortunate enough to be invited into your home will experience your sincere generosity and gracious hospitality first hand. Because of your honest desire to please others, you attract few, if any, enemies in your lifetime.

**DESTINY NUMBER 11 [the higher vibration of the 2]** This is the path of the spiritual and ministerial adviser, counselor, peacemaker, and illuminated public figure. This Destiny master number makes you very sensitive to your surroundings. This high-tuned vibration gives you the capability of readily intuiting others' actions, reactions, and motives, without even being in their presence. In fact, if you allow yourself to "tune in," your psyche can be like a radio receiver. Regardless of whether you tune in or not, you should definitely follow your hunches and take heed of your first impressions. You will discover that a high percentage of your perceptions are right on target! Your congenial style enables you to make and retain friends and companions for a lifetime. As a member of society, you usually feel compelled to contribute selflessly to others in some way. Overall, you are very likeable, gentle, genteel and a complement to the human race. If you don't identify with the attributes of this Master Number, you may acclimate to the number 2, or both. It is good to read both definitions to get a clear picture of what you came to do and be.

**The famous people who have exhibited superlative abilties with the Destiny Numbers 2 and 11:**

**SCIENTISTS:** Neil deGrasse Tyson, Sally Ride, Robert Oppenheimer, (physicist), Lynn Margulis (botanist), Gerty Cori (biochemist), Gerald Edelman (immunologist)

**FINE ARTISTS:** Claude Monet, Lorenzo de Medici, Edouard Manet, Mark Rothko, Marc Chagall, Gustav Klimt, John Constable;

**WRITERS:** Edgar Allan Poe, Jules Verne, Alice Walker, Willa Cather, Judy Blume, Beatrix Potter, Hans Christian Andersen, Jack Kerouac, Philip Roth, Margaret Mitchell

**ATHLETES:** Michael Jordan, Kobe Bryant, Joe Montana, Pete Sampras, Barry Sanders, Conor McGregor, Jim Brown

**MUSICIANS/SINGERS:** Wolfgang Mozart, Tony Bennett, Julie Andrews, Jose Feliciano, LeAnn Rimes., Madonna, Mariah Carey, Shania Twain, Gwen Stefani, Diana Ross, Patti LaBelle, Karen Carpenter, Mick Jagger, Donna Summer, Jennifer Lopez

**COMEDIANS:** Bob Hope, Jack Benny, Jackie Mason, Freddie Prinze, Steven Wright, Jay Leno, Sam Kinison, Damon Wayans, Jeff Foxworthy

**FASHION DESIGNERS:** Coco Chanel, Vera Wang, Miuccia Prada, Issey Miyake, Pierre Balmain

**FAMOUS CHEFS:** Wolfgang Puck, Martin Yan, Mauro Colagreco, Fannie Farmer, Michel Roux, Guy Fieri

**ACTORS:** Ann-Margret, Julie Andrews, Maggie Smith, Kathy Bates, Jessica Lange, Robert Duvall, Gary Oldman, Mark Wahlberg, Richard Burton

**Destiny Number 3:** The path of the adventurous, proverbial "Peter Pan," lover of the arts and pleasure, and/or a highly disciplined, fastidious, linear-oriented professional. If you have a Three Destiny, you are fated to have good fortune throughout your life. That's right – no matter how you might be manifesting this Destiny number, there will always be a helping hand or a windfall that will come your way – even in the eleventh hour when all may seem lost. Regardless of whether you use your Three Destiny to travel the world from a lust for adventure and pleasure, or you spend most of your waking hours working on the next scientific invention that will save the world, you tend to be quite enchanted with life and with your field of endeavor. You are also drawn to the arts and anything that has to do with entertainment. You have a somewhat childlike approach to life that enables you to conjure up ways to make life exciting and adventuresome, or at the very least, enjoyable. You like to function as independently as possible and, along with your joie de vivre qualities, you can be some of most disciplined, dedicated, and intense in any career undertaking.

**The famous people who have exhibited superlative abilties with the Destiny Number 3:**

**SCIENTISTS:** James Watson, Niels Bohr, George Washington Carver, Edwin Hubble, John Forbes Nash, Juliane Koepcke, Robert Koch

**FINE ARTISTS:** Salvador Dali, Albrecht Durer, Umberto Boccioni, Lucia Fontana, El Lissitzky

**WRITERS:** Charles Dickens, Jane Austen, F. Scott Fitzgerald, Franz Kafka, C.S. Lewis, Andre Gide, Gore Vidal, Henry Miller

**ATHLETES:** Jim Thorpe, Sugar Ray Robinson, Ted Williams, Mia Hamm, Julius Erving, Phil Mickelson, Wilt Chamberlain, Maria Sharapova, Jimmy Johnson

**MUSICIANS/SINGERS:** David Bowie, Rihanna, Katy Perry, Christina Aguilera, Kelly Clarkson, Ed Sheeran, Mary J. Blige, Merle Haggard, Rod Stewart, Carlos Santana, Celine Dion, Nina Simone

**COMEDIANS:** Chris Rock, Jon Stewart, Sarah Silverman, Kevin Hart, Joan Rivers, Larry David, Ricky Gervais, Jonathan Winters, Billy Crystal, Alan King, Wanda Sykes

**FASHION DESIGNERS:** Jimmy Choo, Yohji Yamamoto, Mary Quant, Rihanna, Riccardo Tisci

**FAMOUS CHEFS:** Joel Robuchon, Rachel Ray, Jacques Pepin

**ACTORS:** Helen Hayes, Audrey Hepburn, Jodie Foster, Brie Larson, Robert Redford, Liam Neeson, Jeff Bridges, Alec Guinness, Jamie Foxx

**Destiny Number 4:** The path of the hard-working, kind-hearted, honest, and dedicated "Rock of Gibraltar," the Four Destiny contains such a super-charged vibration that it could turn you into a success with a capital S! Like your Four Destiny counterparts Microsoft founders Bill Gates and Paul Allen, Oprah Winfrey, and Google founders Sergey Brin and Larry Page, you have the potential to build an empire. You possess a strong work ethic, organizational skills, and the innate determination to constantly better yourself in any career endeavor you choose. Regardless of whether you achieve high honors, experience monumental monetary gains, or live a simple, quiet, hard-working existence, most of you feel compelled to do something to serve or help mankind and the earth. It is the "mission" of those with Four destinies to use your career to help others in some way. That is a natural impulse that goes with your life path, and most of you embrace it wholeheartedly. Regardless of whether you are a homemaker, a forest ranger, a rock star, or a ditch digger, you will give 100%. When you accept a responsibility, you are ready, willing, and able to fulfill its requirements. Honesty and fairness are important to Four Destiny people and you are not inclined to become martyrs or to hold back your true feelings when asked for your opinion on anything.

**Destiny Number 22 [the higher vibration of number 4]:** The path of the master builder, you have the innate power to affect self-mastery, accumulate wealth, and even become famous. Exceptional perceptivity, intelligence, strong moral values, and ethical principles are a few of the qualities possessed by those who have this Destiny number. It is not easy to live up to the high standards required of the 22 because, like the number 11, it calls for a high-minded, spiritually-oriented approach to life. It is important that this power is used for the good of mankind in a humanitarian way in order to accept its highest potential. By embracing that nature, you can receive honors and acclaim during your lifetime for your philanthropic deeds and altruistic nature. If you don't identify with the attributes of this Master Number, you may acclimate to the number 4, or both. It is good to read both definitions to get a clear picture of what you came to do and be.

**The famous people who have exhibited superlative abilties with the Destiny Numbers 4 and 22:**

**SCIENTISTS/PHILOSOPHERS:** Immanuel Kant, Sigmund Freud, Michael Faraday, Francis Crick, Marie Curie, Leonardo da Vinci, Gregor Mendel, Robert Oppenheimer, Kurt Godel

**FINE ARTISTS:** Vincent Van Gogh, Paul Cezanne, El Greco, Jacques-Louis David, Edward Hopper, René Magritte

**WRITERS:** Mark Twain, J.D. Salinger, Will Rogers, Geoffrey Chaucer, Harriet Beecher Stowe, Carl Sandburg, Robert Frost

**ATHLETES:** Babe Ruth, Jim Thorpe, Lou Dorchen, Johnny Bench, Arnold Schwarzenegger, Larry Bird, Martina Navratilova, Deion Sanders, Mike Tyson, Nadia Comaneci

**MUSICIANS/SINGERS:** Nat King Cole, Isaac Stern, Charlie Parker, Miles Davis, Willie Nelson, Luciano Pavarotti, Neil Diamond, Itzhak Perlman, Elton John, Seal, Paul McCartney, Dolly Parton, Frank Sinatra

**COMEDIANS:** Lenny Bruce, Don Rickles, Woody Allen, Shelley Berman, Roseanne Barr, Adam Sandler, Bill Burr

**FASHION DESIGNERS:** Stella McCartney, Carolina Herrera

**FAMOUS CHEFS:** Paul Bocuse, Emeril Lagasse, Marco Pierre White

**ACTORS:** Vivien Leigh, Anne Bancroft, Helen Hunt, Hilary Swank, Nicole Kidman, Oprah Winfrey, Julianne Moore, William Holden, John Wayne, Clint Eastwood, Tom Selleck, Steve McQueen, Woody Allen, Robert Downey, Jr., Russell Crowe, Quentin Tarantino, Matthew McConaughey, Brad Pitt

**Destiny Number 5:** The Number 5 destiny is the path of the freedom fighter and energized, stylish mover-shakers. Having a Five Destiny, you are highly adaptable and desiring of constant change, diversity, and activity. Always on the go, usually in the fast lane, you move from place to place in record time. You like to dress in the latest fashions, tackle your business and personal obligations with unparalleled vim, vigor, and efficiency, and still have energy reserves to participate in an active social and/or athletic life. You are neat, tidy, and competent. Even though you usually have multiple projects and even volunteer for more, you will drop what you're doing to help someone in need. You are the consummate social participant, the all-around good guy and gal. You are an excellent promoter, networker, organizer, and orchestrator, and when inspired or motivated by a cause, you are an unbeatable fundraiser. Chameleon-like in nature, you are drawn to people of diverse cultures and backgrounds. This Destiny number makes it easy for you to be a team player. You don't need to be the head honcho or in the limelight, though many of you end up there because you are so well liked, efficient, and a capable leader.

**The famous people who have exhibited superlative abilties with the Destiny Number 5:**

**SCIENTISTS:** Charles Darwin, Benjamin Franklin, Dian Fossey, Linus Pauling, Louis Braille, Maria Goeppert-Mayer

**FINE ARTISTS:** Pierre-Auguste Renoir, William Blake, Maxime Du Camp, Georgia O'Keeffe

**WRITERS:** James Joyce, William Faulkner, John Steinbeck, Arthur Conan Doyle, Albert Camus, Tennessee Williams, Hermann Hesse, Harper Lee, Barbara Kingsolver, Malcolm X

**ATHLETES:** Kareem Abdul Jabbar, Willie McCovey, Jerry Rice, Floyd Mayweather, Billie Jean King, Andre Agassi, Venus Williams, Cathy Rigby, Michael Phelps

**MUSICIANS/SINGERS:** Louis Armstrong, Hank Williams, John Coltrane, Mick Jagger, Jon Bon Jovi, Kurt Cobain, George Michael, Tina Turner, Jay-Z, Beyoncé, Tina Turner, Dr. Dre, Bruno Mars

**COMEDIANS:** Andy Kaufman, Ellen DeGeneres, Conan O'Brien, Johnny Carson, Margaret Cho, John Cleese, Dennis Miller, Albert Brooks, Martin Lawrence

**FASHION DESIGNERS:** Marc Jacobs, Michael Kors, Pierre Cardin, Anna Sui, Isaac Mizrahi

**FAMOUS CHEFS:** James Beard, Gordon Ramsay, Alice Waters, Tom Colicchio, Alain Chapel, Steven Raichlen, Charles Trotter, Judy Rodgers

**ACTORS:** Joan Fontaine, Joan Crawford, Julie Christie, Jessica Tandy, Angelina Jolie, Clark Gable, Gary Cooper, Robert Mitchum, Marlon Brando, Sidney Poitier, Jeremy Irons, Ron Howard, Denzel Washington, Sean Penn

**Destiny Number 6:** The Number 6 Destiny is the path of the responsible, honorable, good citizen and cosmic parent to all. Those of you with a Six Destiny are some of the most caring humans on the planet. You are principled and patient, conscientious and careful, home-lovers and hospitable, devoted, and dedicated to your family, friends, jobs, and your favorite causes. You have exceptional teaching and managerial skills and you are given many opportunities to showcase these talents because of your innate desire to help and be of service. You are the best pet owners and plant/garden tenders, and you are usually the first to volunteer to help those who have difficulty helping themselves. When on the job, you are the type who goes the extra mile – finding more things to do that you know need to be done, even things that aren't part of your job description. All of you are social. You enjoy the company of family and friends and also attending community events and social gatherings. There IS no better or more devoted friend and employee than someone with a Six Destiny, and you nurture your friendships on a constant basis. Most of you are romantics and openly affectionate.

**The famous people who have exhibited superlative abilties with the Destiny Number 6:**

**SCIENTISTS:** Galileo Galilei, Thomas Edison, Albert Einstein, Robert Boyle, Lisa Meitner, Alan Turing, Jane Goodall

**FINE ARTISTS:** Donatello, Henri Matisse, Jackson Pollock, Edgar Degas, Caravaggio, Edvard Munch, Willem de Kooning

**WRITERS:** Elizabeth Barrett Browning, Lewis Carroll, J.R.R. Tolkien, H. G Wells, Edith Wharton, Agatha Christie, Stephen King, Charles Schulz, Ian Fleming

**ATHLETES:** Hank Aaron, Sandy Koufax, John Madden, Barry Bonds, Joe DiMaggio, Terry Bradshaw, Drew Brees, Bjorn Borg

**MUSICIANS/SINGERS:** B.B. King, Beverly Sills, Michael Jackson, Steve Tyler, Stevie Wonder, John Lennon, Linda Ronstadt, Brian Wilson, Gladys Knight, Britney Spears

**COMEDIANS:** Billy Connolly, Phyllis Diller, Steve Martin, Bill Maher, Eddie Murphy, Norm Macdonald, Lewis Black

**FASHION DESIGNERS:** Hubert de Givenchy, Bill Blass, Victoria Beckham

**FAMOUS CHEFS:** Bobby Flay, Joan Roca i Fontané, Alain Passard

**ACTORS:** Vanessa Redgrave, Claire Danes,–Mary Tyler Moore, Joanne Woodward, Ellen Burstyn, Sissy Spacek, Meryl Streep, Frances McDormand, Jennifer Lawrence, Cary Grant, James Dean, Robert DeNiro, Michael Caine, Ben Kingsley, Sylvester Stallone, Bruce Willis, Don Cheadle

**Destiny Number 7:** The 7 Destiny is the path of the scholar, the perfectionist, and the keeper of secrets. Dignity is the most important element of your existence. You are loath to bring unwanted attention to yourself or to make yourself look foolish in any way. For those reasons, most of you learn at an early age to listen rather than talk. You are not meddlesome people and do not seek personal information from others – even those closest to you. Although you don't pry into the lives of others because you dislike anyone asking you about your personal business, many people open up to you and sometimes offer you their most intimate secrets. This is because they sense by your own private nature that you will keep theirs private too. Almost everyone with a Seven Destiny is a perfectionist in one way or another. You definitely bring a motivation for perfection to your career. You enjoy researching and analyzing and if your chosen work is in medicine, the law, or high tech, your favorite part would be gathering the facts and analyzing your findings. You have broad and ever-expanding interests in the sciences, philosophies, the arts and the mysteries of life and the world. People with 7 Destinies are sometimes considered odd or unusual, but the 7 is the number of genius, mastery, truth-seeking, and ingenuity and it's those qualities that shine through.

**The famous people who have exhibited superlative abilties with the have exhibited superlative abilties with the Destiny Number 7**:

**SCIENTISTS:** Stephen Hawking, Louis Pasteur, Norman Borlaug (Green Revolution), Pierre Curie (radioactivity), Barbara McClintock (geneticist). Buzz Aldrin, Neil Armstrong

**FINE ARTISTS:** Paul Gauguin, Andy Warhol, Francisco Goya, James Whistler

**WRITERS:** Fyodor Dostoyevsky, Toni Morrison, Marcel Proust, George Elliott, Emily Dickinson, Sylvia Plath, Gertrude Stein, Arthur Miller, Edith Wharton, George Bernard Shaw, William F. Buckley

**ATHLETES:** Willie Mays, Yogi Berra, Reggie Jackson, Jackie Joyner-Kersee, Novak Djokovic, Chris Evert Lloyd, Arthur Ashe, Mohammed Ali, Bruce Lee, Carl Lewis, Stephen Curry

**MUSICIANS/SINGERS:** Johann Bach, Peter Tchaikovsky, Ludwig van Beethoven, Frederic Chopin, Franz Liszt, Leonard Bernstein, Johnny Cash, Joe Cocker, John Fogerty, Jerry Garcia, Eric Clapton, Freddie Mercury, Carrie Underwood, Taylor Swift, Janet Jackson, Pink

**COMEDIANS:** Jerry Seinfeld, Dave Chappelle, David Brenner, Larry Miller, Mel Brooks

**FASHION DESIGNERS:** Giorgio Armani, Tom Ford, Donna Karan, Gianni Versace, Zac Posen, Betsey Johnson

**FAMOUS CHEFS:** Alain Ducasse, Anthony Bourdain, Mar Bittman, Sanjeev Kapoor, Edna Lewis

**ACTORS:** Michael Douglas, Leonardo DiCaprio, Al Pacino, Johnny Depp, Mel Gibson, James Stewart, Peter O'Toole, Peter Sellers, Burt Lancaster, Michael Douglas, Christian Bale, Martin Sheen, John Goodman, Katherine Hepburn, Marilyn Monroe, Emma Thompson, Susan Sarandon, Julia Roberts, Helen Mirren, Natalie Portman, Emma Stone

**MISCELLANEOUS:** Winston Churchill, Queen Elizabeth II, Princess Diana, Leslie Stahl

**Destiny Number 8:** The Number 8 is the path of the matriarch/patriarch, judge and jury, producer/director, teacher of teachers, and the class act. No one has more savoir-faire and aplomb than someone with an Eight Destiny. You know how to look good, how to help others look good, and how to make your surroundings look sensational! You never settle for second best where your purchases are concerned, and most of you possess an innate sixth sense with regard to people and ferreting out the best price for the highest quality items. You are the quintessential dreamer of grandiose dreams. Your unshakeable belief in yourself, and your innate and learned talents, along with your willingness to take the chances to make your dreams come true, make you believe you deserve to have more than most, and many of you do. Once you achieve fame and fortune, you don't flaunt your wealth or become pretentious, but rather enjoy championing worthy causes and giving with discrimination and generosity. You are excellent executives, professionals, managers, and entrepreneurs. Whatever position in which you find yourself, you become known for your competence and first-rate efforts.

**The famous people who have exhibited superlative abilties with the Destiny Number 8:**

**SCIENTISTS:** Nicolaus Copernicus, Alexander Graham Bell, Richard Feynman, Richard Dawkins, Jonas Salk, Timothy Leary, Alan Shepard

**FINE ARTISTS:** Michelangelo, Raphael, Pablo Picasso, Rembrandt, Gustave Courbet, Johannes Vermeer, Winslow Homer

**WRITERS:** George Orwell, Oscar Wilde, Mary Shelley, Ezra Pound, Jack London, James Baldwin, Rudyard Kipling

**ATHLETES:** Wayne Gretzky, Jesse Owens, Babe Zaharias, Aaron Rodgers, Mickey Mantle, Derek Jeter, Roger Federer, Usain Bolt, Tom Brady, Venus Williams

**MUSICIANS/SINGERS:** Aretha Franklin, Amy Winehouse, Johann S. Bach, Bob Dylan, Aretha Franklin, Stevie Nicks, Joni Mitchell, Jessica Simpson

**COMEDIANS:** Dana Carvey, Louis C.K., Robin Williams, Amy Schumer, Bob Newhart, Ben Stiller, Whoopi Goldberg, Robert Klein, Redd Foxx, Mort Sahl, Henny Youngman

**FASHION DESIGNERS:** Karl Lagerfeld, Oscar de la Renta, Alber Elbaz

**FAMOUS CHEFS:** Martha Stewart, Thomas Keller, Mario Batali, Michael Bras, Ina Garten, Eric Ripert

**ACTORS:** Paul Newman, Gene Hackman, Jon Voight, Gregory Peck, Gene Kelly, Laurence Olivier, Robin Williams, Philip Seymour Hoffman, Colin Firth, Benicio del Toro, Blair Underwood, Matt Damon, Ben Stiller, Elizabeth Taylor, Barbra Streisand, Jane Fonda, Liza Minnelli, Diane Keaton, Sandra Bullock, Cate Blanchett, Penelope Cruz

**MISCELLANEOUS:** General Douglas MacArthur, Dick Clark, Diane Sawyer

**Destiny Number 9:** The Number 9 Destiny is the path of the "old soul" and universal humanitarian. Having a Nine Destiny, you possess a naturally refined and aristocratic bearing. Most of you knew from an early age that you wanted to do something grand with your life. You are drawn to the finest things, from Cartier jewelry and caviar to Bentleys and butlers. There lurks within you, however, a strong motivation to do something far-reaching that helps the masses through charity or philanthropy. Being an "old soul", you have ready access to your past life knowledge. Because this innate information is so accessible, you simply know things you've never studied, and therefore many of you may sometimes feel that you are not given the respect or acknowledgement you deserve. Being an older and therefore possibly wiser soul, your mission with the Nine Destiny is to be more humane, humble, and giving than most others. Respect is earned on the earth plane through actions, accomplishments, and demeanor, and you will gain the acknowledgment you desire by exhibiting your charm, wit and people-pleasing demeanor, along with your great reservoir of knowledge and talents, in the pursuit of humanitarian endeavors.

**The famous people who have exhibited superlative abilties with the Destiny Number 9**:

**SCIENTISTS:** John Logie Baird (electrical engineer – "Father of TV"), Leon Lederman (physicist), Omar Khayyam (astronomer), Emmy Noether (mathematician), Rita Levi-Montalcini (neurologist), Peggy Whitson (astronomy), Joseph Lister (surgeon/scientist), Alan Kay (computer science), Harold Urcy

**FINE ARTISTS:** Sandro Botticelli, Paul Rubens, Henri de Toulouse-Lautrec, Franz Marc, Joan Miro, David Hockney, Maxim Gorky, Gustave Moreau

**WRITERS:** Virginia Woolf, Kurt Vonnegut, Gustave Flaubert, Tom Wolfe, Louisa May Alcott, Allen Ginsberg, Anne Frank, Orson Welles, John Keats, Anton Chekhov, Anais Nin, Henry David Thoreau

**ATHLETES:** Sam Snead, Bobby Orr, Leon Spinks, Steffi Graf, Serena Williams, Jack Nicklaus, Mark Spitz, Brett Favre, Michael Johnson, Rory McIlroy

**MUSICIANS/SINGERS:** Billie Holiday, Elvis Presley, Jimi Hendrix, Ray Charles, Cole Porter, Henri Mancini, Whitney Houston, Adele, Alicia Keys, Justin Bieber, Ariana Grande, Cher, Alicia Keys

**COMEDIANS:** W. C. Fields, Mae West, Richard Pryor, Bernie Mac, Mel Brooks, Eddie Izzard, George Burns, Garry Shandling, Flip Wilson

**FASHION DESIGNERS:** Alexander McQueen, Jean-Paul Gaultier, Donatella Versace, Christian Louboutin, Narciso Rodriguez, Tory Burch

**FAMOUS CHEFS:** Julia Child, Jamie Oliver, Heston Blumenthal, Nobu Matsuhisa, René Redzepi, Albert Roux

**ACTORS:** Eddie Redmayne, Harrison Ford, Morgan Freeman, Anthony Hopkins, Henry Fonda, Dustin Hoffman, Jack Lemmon, Jim Carrey, Bill Murray, Shirley MacLaine, Halle Berry, Sharon Stone

**MISCELLANEOUS:** Erté, Norman Rockwell, Charles Lindbergh, Paramhansa Yogananda, Mahatma Gandhi, Mother Teresa, Spike Lee, Tyra Banks, Malala Yousafzai, President Jimmy Carter

## MOTHER TERESA'S NUMBER COMPILATIONS:

CHARACTER NUMBER = 8
The Chairman of the Board; the Exemplar

DESTINY NUMBER = 9
The Universal Humanitarian

PERSONALITY NUMBER = 8
The Chairman of the Board, the Exemplar

## NELSON MANDELA'S NUMBER COMPILATIONS:

CHARACTER NUMBER = 9
Universal humanitarian

DESTINY NUMBER = 8
The Exemplar, Commander, Teacher of Teachers

PERSONALITY NUMBER = 9
Universal Humanitarian, Advanced Soul

## THE DALAI LAMA'S NUMBER COMPILATIONS:

(Birth Name: Lhamo Thondup)

CHARACTER NUMBER = 3
The Creative Communicator

DESTINY NUMBER = 22
Builder of Empires; Social/Spiritual Leader

PERSONALITY NUMBER = 6
The Humanitarian, Exemplary Teacher/Human Being

## OPRAH WINFREY'S NUMBER COMPILATIONS:

CHARACTER NUMBER = 6
The Humanitarian, Exemplary Parent/Teacher/
Human Being

DESTINY NUMBER = 22
Builder of Empires; Social/Spiritual Leader

PERSONALITY NUMBER = 11
Empathetic/Intuitive Social Leader

## MUHAMMED ALI'S NUMBER COMPILATIONS:

(Birth Name: Cassius Marcellus Clay)

CHARACTER NUMBER = 3
The Creative Communicator

DESTINY NUMBER = 7
The Genius and Perfectionist

PERSONALITY NUMBER = 8
The Exemplar, Commander-in-Chief.

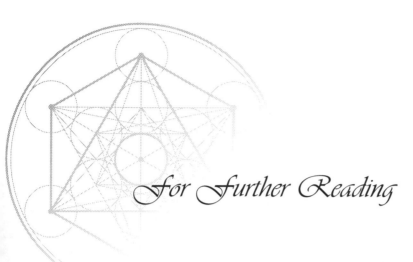

# For Further Reading

*The Spirit of Gaia* and

*Insights from the Other Side* by Mellen-Thomas Benedict

*Sacred Science of Numbers* by Corinne Heline

*Our Ultimate Reality* by Adrian P. Cooper

*The Tao of Physics* by Fritjof Capra

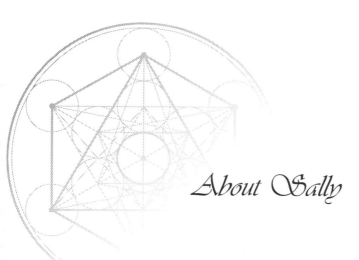

# About Sally

**S** **ALLY FAUBION** is a numerology expert with over 50 years of helping thousands of individuals use the metaphysical sciences to improve their lives, families, businesses, and organizations. Sally is based in San Francisco, where she made a name for herself as one of the most sought-after spiritual advisors in the community. Her vast experience and passion for numerology make her a go-to for individuals, celebrities, Fortune 500 corporations, and well-known organizations looking to better understand the mystical science of numerology.

**AUTHOR** Sally's first book, *Motivational Numerology: How Numbers Affect Your Life* (Seven Locks Press, 2001), has earned praise from readers. It is available for purchase on her website and on Amazon. Her second book, *What Makes My Child Tick?: Numerology Delivers the Answers*, is available on Amazon in both print and Kindle formats. In addition to her books, Sally was the writer for metaphysical content for Teen Magazine for several years, including a popular numerology column. Sally also wrote metaphysical content for gaming technology companies Activision and Girl Games.

**PROFESSIONAL SPEAKER, ENTERTAINER** Sally is frequently commissioned to speak and entertain for audiences and organizations of all sizes, performing at small, intimate gatherings and large corporate events. Clients include organizations such as Apple,

Genentech, Oracle, the City of San Francisco, Macy's, Neiman Marcus, Old Navy, The San Francisco Junior League, St. Francis Yacht Club, Silver Springs Country Club, Countryside Health Spa, and U.S. Military Medical Officers, among others. Her charismatic presence and thorough content are valued by her audiences, and she is frequently called back for repeat performances by her clients. Entertainment varies from speaking to the history and significance of numerology to analyzing employees and perform team-building activities.

Sally's core passion is working with individuals to help them attain perspective about their lives, make better decisions, and maximize their potential. Sally's readings combine her intuition and expert knowledge of numerology backed by years of knowledge and purpose. Learn to appreciate and respect who you have come onto this planet to be and do – book a reading with Sally today! Just visit www. sallysnumbers.com.

Printed in the United States
By Bookmasters